CONTENTS

INTRODUCTION

Life has its ups and downs, and knowing how to adapt to adversity is essential to our health and happiness. Resilience is the ability to bounce back from the difficulties we all face. The good news is that psychologists have identified methods and strategies that enable us to navigate through crisis and overcome misfortune. You don't have to be a self-help guru to be resilient – it is within us all. By making some small changes to your lifestyle, and by thinking positively, you can weather whatever storms come your way. This book is packed with simple tips, inspirational statements and encouraging quotations to help you build your inner strength and tackle the tough times with hope and resolve.

HOW TO BE
RESILIENT

ANNA BARNES

vie

An Hachette UK Company
www.hachette.co.uk

Vie Books, an imprint of Summersdale Publishers Ltd
Part of Octopus Publishing Group Limited
Carmelite House
50 Victoria Embankment
LONDON
EC4Y 0DZ
UK

www.summersdale.com

Printed and bound in Croatia

ISBN: 978-1-78685-514-5

Substantial discounts on bulk quantities of Summersdale books are available
to corporations, professional associations and other organisations. For
details contact general enquiries: telephone: +44 (0) 1243 771107 or email:
enquiries@summersdale.com.

RESILIENCE FOR EVERY DAY

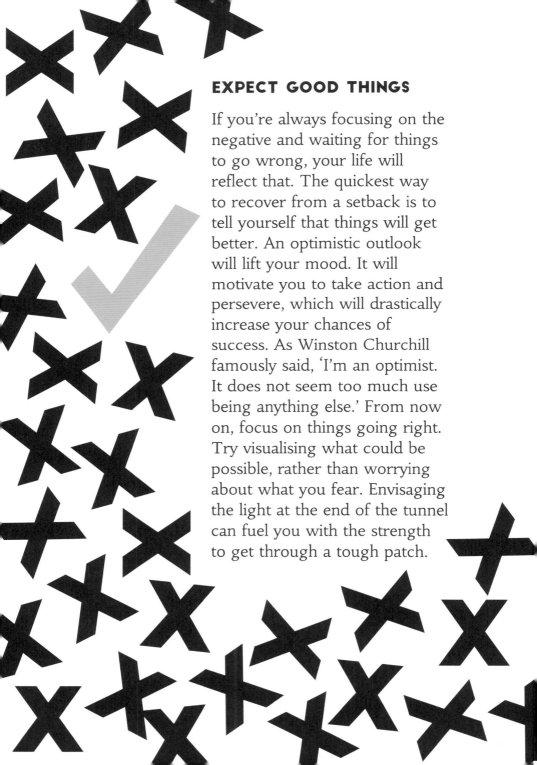

EXPECT GOOD THINGS

If you're always focusing on the negative and waiting for things to go wrong, your life will reflect that. The quickest way to recover from a setback is to tell yourself that things will get better. An optimistic outlook will lift your mood. It will motivate you to take action and persevere, which will drastically increase your chances of success. As Winston Churchill famously said, 'I'm an optimist. It does not seem too much use being anything else.' From now on, focus on things going right. Try visualising what could be possible, rather than worrying about what you fear. Envisaging the light at the end of the tunnel can fuel you with the strength to get through a tough patch.

WHATEVER GOOD THINGS WE BUILD END UP BUILDING US.

JIM ROHN

GET COMFORTABLE WITH BEING UNCOMFORTABLE

Life isn't easy and there will be many struggles along the way, such as confronting big events like moving home or when we experience the loss of a friendship. Some people accept that change is part of life and find it easier to deal with. They understand that in order for things to improve, they may need to go through some discomfort and uncertainty – whether that's going to job interviews or meeting a financial advisor to sort out their money troubles. For others, change is a real challenge. You can build up your resilience by stepping outside of

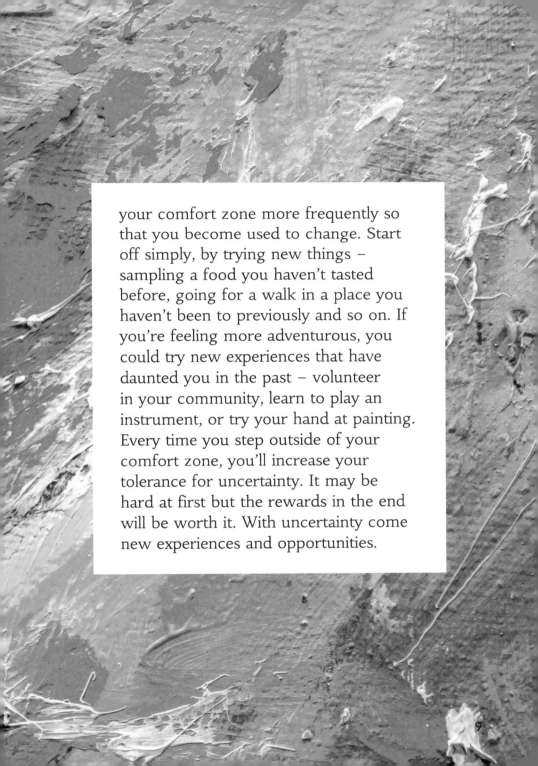

your comfort zone more frequently so that you become used to change. Start off simply, by trying new things – sampling a food you haven't tasted before, going for a walk in a place you haven't been to previously and so on. If you're feeling more adventurous, you could try new experiences that have daunted you in the past – volunteer in your community, learn to play an instrument, or try your hand at painting. Every time you step outside of your comfort zone, you'll increase your tolerance for uncertainty. It may be hard at first but the rewards in the end will be worth it. With uncertainty come new experiences and opportunities.

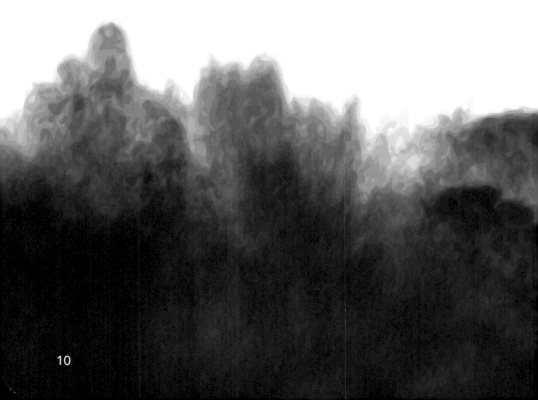

STRUGGLES LEAD TO STRENGTH

The strongest tree in the forest is not the one that is protected from the wind and rain. The strongest trees are those that are exposed to the elements. They develop deep roots and stout trunks in order to survive. In the same way, the struggles we face and overcome in life make us stronger. Reminding yourself of this fact can help you weather the storms of life.

THE BAMBOO
THAT BENDS
IS STRONGER
THAN THE OAK
THAT RESISTS.

JAPANESE PROVERB

RESILIENCE ISN'T ABOUT HOW MUCH SUFFERING YOU CAN TAKE

If you are struggling with some aspect of your life, take a step back and approach the problem from a different angle. Imagine you are looking at the issue through a different lens. After a bit of reflection you might be surprised by how inconsequential your concern now seems.

Whatever the present moment contains, accept it as if you had chosen it.

ECKHART TOLLE

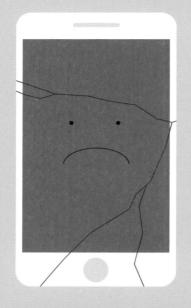

CHOOSE YOUR RESPONSE

We all experience bad days and crises in our lives, but how we respond to these situations is up to us. When something 'bad' happens, we can choose to react negatively, or we can opt to remain calm and look for a solution. We often fall into the habit of reacting to situations in the same way. It's important to realise that the way you react is up to you. When faced with a setback, pause for a moment and consciously decide how you would like to respond. So, next time you drop your phone and smash the screen think, *it's very annoying, but it can be repaired* and *that will cost, so I'll have to cut back on something to afford it, but it's not the end of the world.*

Happiness is a journey, not a destination

FIND YOUR CALLING

A sense of purpose can enable us to overcome challenges that might otherwise overwhelm us. It can give us the determination to keep going, despite discomfort. This is best summed up by a quote from the philosopher Nietzsche: 'He who has a why to live can bear almost any how.' To find your purpose, identify what you're drawn to. Which moments make you feel authentic, as if you are doing something you were truly made for?

Perhaps
you have
experienced
this feeling when
organising an event,
looking after an
animal or child, writing
a letter to a friend or
creating a work of art.
You may have also experienced
'flow' – a state in which you're so
immersed in what you're doing that
time seems to disappear. Look at what
gives your life meaning and trust what
your heart tells you. A strong sense of
purpose will fill you with motivation
and enthusiasm, and help you to
transcend the ups and downs of life.

BREATHE INTO TENSION

If you encounter a difficult situation today, notice which parts of your body feel tense and breathe into the area to help you relax. For example, if you carry tension in your shoulders, feel your breath filling your lungs, expanding your chest and try to let your shoulder muscles relax and send your breath to that area of your body. Remind yourself that challenging moments always pass. For example, if you realise you might miss your bus and therefore will be late, as you rush to get to the bus stop your adrenalin levels will rise making you feel nervous. However, that adrenalin will help you speed up and catch the bus, and the uncomfortable feeling will disperse once you are on your way.

STAND FIRM, LIKE A TREE

A great way to take control when you're in the midst of turmoil and feel like you might be swept away by it all is to mentally ground yourself. Press your feet to the ground and visualise roots growing from your soles into the ground. Take some deep breaths, making time to feel the air entering your lungs and then slowly release it. Stand firm like a tree, while the chaos around you blows through your branches and disappears in the breeze.

Make today a 'NO RUSH' day

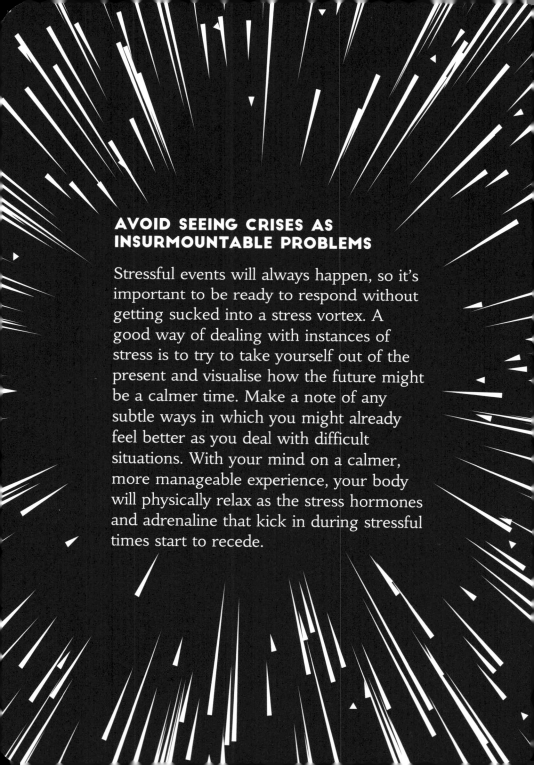

AVOID SEEING CRISES AS INSURMOUNTABLE PROBLEMS

Stressful events will always happen, so it's important to be ready to respond without getting sucked into a stress vortex. A good way of dealing with instances of stress is to try to take yourself out of the present and visualise how the future might be a calmer time. Make a note of any subtle ways in which you might already feel better as you deal with difficult situations. With your mind on a calmer, more manageable experience, your body will physically relax as the stress hormones and adrenaline that kick in during stressful times start to recede.

WHETHER YOU THINK
YOU CAN
OR YOU THINK
YOU CAN'T,
YOU'RE RIGHT.

HENRY FORD

A
RESILIENT
MIND

OUR MINDS ARE LIKE OUR STOMACHS; THEY ARE WHETTED BY THE CHANGE OF THEIR FOOD, AND VARIETY SUPPLIES BOTH WITH FRESH APPETITE.

QUINTILIAN

MENTAL FORTITUDE IS DEVELOPED

We all want to be mentally stronger. But mental toughness isn't simply something you're born with – it is learnt from experience, practised and developed over time. Just as our physical selves can be made stronger with exercise and a good diet, so too can your mental strength, by using the techniques that follow as a 'workout' for your mind.

WHEN'S THE BEST TIME TO START?

NOW! NOW! NOW! NOW! NOW! NOW!

LOOK FOR THE SILVER LINING

Mentally strong people have the ability to see the positives in tough circumstances and they recognise that it is possible for good things to come from hardship. This doesn't erase the hardship, but it can make it easier to cope with. The next time you face a challenge, ask yourself, 'What can I learn from this? What is this an opportunity for? How can this positively affect me?'

HAPPY WITH

THINGS I WOULD LIKE TO CHANGE

FUTURE

WRITE A LETTER TO YOURSELF

Although this might seem like a strange idea at first, sometimes writing things down is an effective way of settling your thoughts and organising your mind, and this process can be very cathartic. Taking the time to sit down and write yourself a letter – in which you spell out what you are happy with, the things you would like to change and what you would like to do in the future – can help you come to terms with aspects of yourself that are making you feel uncertain or worried. It can also help to move your focus to the future and the positive work you can do to feel better about yourself.

LIGHTEN UP

Seeing the funny side of life can help you rise above painful situations. You might be one of those people who struggles to see the lighter side and is wired to view life through a more serious lens. Don't worry – you can train your brain to see the lighter side. If you're struggling, take a step back in order to gain some perspective. Try not to take yourself too seriously and note the absurd or ironic things that happen to you. A sense of humour won't cure all your problems, but it will make them a lot easier to deal with.

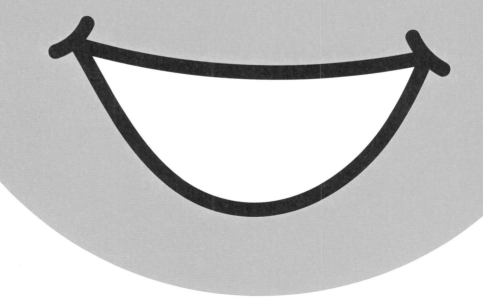

BELIEVE IT!

Try to find alternative perspectives on life. If you alter the lens through which you view things it can have a big impact. For example, when you adopt a new, empowering belief with absolute certainty, you can accomplish virtually anything. Here are five inspiring beliefs to try out:

THERE IS ALWAYS A WAY IF I'M COMMITTED.

THE PAST DOES NOT EQUAL THE FUTURE.

EVERY NEW EXPERIENCE MAKES ME STRONGER.

THERE ARE NO FAILURES - ONLY OUTCOMES I CAN LEARN FROM.

I CREATE MY OWN LIFE.

WHEN YOU HAVE EXHAUSTED
ALL POSSIBILITIES, REMEMBER
THIS: YOU HAVEN'T.

THOMAS EDISON

34

NOBODY CAN HOLD YOU BACK!

TAKE THE BULL BY THE HORNS

Instead of hiding away from potentially
difficult situations, try to confront
them head on. Make decisive
decisions rather than avoiding the
problem and hoping it goes away.

BE HOPEFUL

Instead of worrying about what you fear, visualise what you want. This will help you cultivate a positive outlook on life.

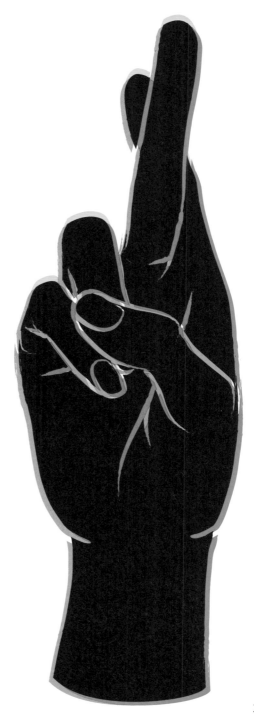

Life isn't about
waiting for the
storm to pass;
it's about learning
to dance in the rain.

Anonymous

IT'S YOUR CHOICE

People with good mental strength take responsibility for their lives. They don't blame other people for 'making them feel bad' or 'messing up their day'. Instead, they take control of their own thoughts, feelings and behaviour. They understand that life isn't always easy or fair, but they don't sit around feeling sorry for themselves. Resilient people acknowledge that everything they do – from the time they wake up until the time they go to sleep at night – is a choice.

BE A CHILD AGAIN TODAY.

AND SPREAD SOME MISCHIEF!

LEARN FROM YOUR SETBACKS

Even bad experiences have worth. Start seeing what lessons you can take from negative situations and consider those lessons gifts from the universe. After all, if you never failed, how would you ever learn to be resilient? The most successful people in life have all suffered many setbacks, but one thing they have in common is that they learned from those setbacks.

KEEP CALM AND CARRY ON

One of the most important keys to resilience during tough times is to control your emotions. It's very easy to get swept away by what is happening and slip into negative thinking. Resilient people are able to remain calm and focused, despite the turmoil that may be surrounding them. One of the best ways to build this skill is to practise remaining calm and focused in everyday situations. If you practise on the little things, calmness will become a habit that will kick in when you need it most. The next time your train is late, or your bag breaks and empties your shopping all over the floor, try remaining cool and calm. The regular practice of yoga, meditation or mindfulness can also help you with this.

FACE REALITY

No one is immune to setbacks. They happen to everyone. The question is, when misfortune occurs, do you waste time and energy resisting what is happening or do you put all your energy into doing what you can to move forward? If you find yourself regularly thinking things like, *I shouldn't have to deal with this* and *why me?* you may be fighting reality. Resilient people accept the reality they are faced with, even if it's uncomfortable, and focus all their energy on changing the circumstance or improving their coping abilities.

YOU'VE GOT THIS!

TEND TO YOUR SELF-ESTEEM

Remind yourself of your strengths
and what you have achieved. Think
of the challenges you have faced
so far that you have overcome – if
you could beat them, you can beat
whatever else life throws at you.

All You Have To Do Is Try.

TELL A DIFFERENT STORY

While we can't control exactly what happens in life, we can control what we tell ourselves about what's happened. Emotionally robust people have the ability to reframe situations, even when they seem challenging or scary. By looking for value and meaning in stressful events they are able to see 'bad' experiences in a positive light. For example, instead of seeing obstacles as stopping you from achieving your goals, you see them as opportunities to adapt and grow. Instead of fearing failure, you see failure as a necessary stepping stone on the way to success. Reframing is a powerful way to transform your thinking and boost your mental toughness. It won't change the situation, but it will put things into a healthier perspective and keep you motivated to carry on. Try it and see what a big difference it makes.

THE POWER OF RESILIENCE

WHAT'S YOUR EXPLANATION?

The way you explain life's setbacks to yourself is important. Psychologists say that an optimistic (and therefore more resilient) 'explanatory style' is composed of three main elements. Firstly, optimistic people view the effects of bad events as being temporary rather than permanent. For example, instead of saying, 'My boss never thanks me for my hard work,' they might say, 'My boss didn't thank me for my hard work on that project.' Secondly, resilient people don't let setbacks affect unrelated areas of their life. For instance, they would say, 'I'm not the best at cooking,' rather than, 'I'm no good at anything.' Finally, resilient people don't blame themselves unnecessarily when bad events occur. They think rationally to determine the cause. So, if they get made redundant, they are likely to say, 'The company doesn't have much work at the moment,' rather than, 'I wasn't good at my job!' People with an optimistic explanatory style tend to be happier, healthier and more successful at work, school and in sport. Those with a pessimistic explanatory style are more prone to depression, anxiety and low self-esteem.

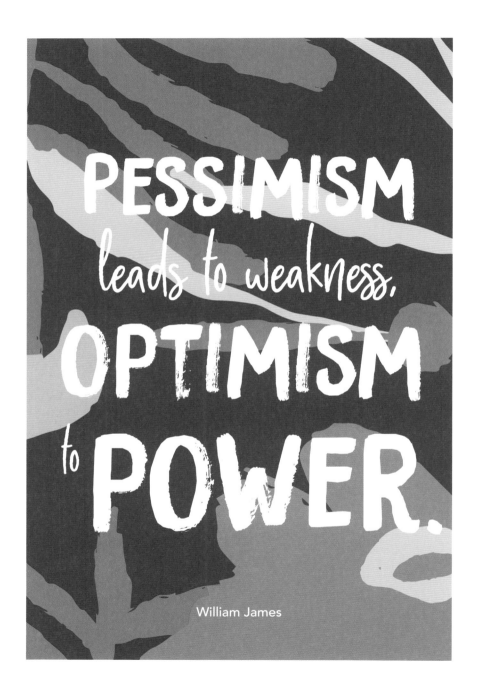

PESSIMISM *leads to weakness,* OPTIMISM *to* POWER.

William James

WHEN LIFE GIVES YOU LEMONS...

If you're stuck in a traffic jam on your way to work, how do you react? Do you accept the situation and take advantage of the extra time to listen to the radio, or do you tense up and sink into a bad mood? Whichever way you react, it won't change the situation. Resilient people make the most of whatever they are faced with. In this way, a traffic jam becomes an opportunity rather than a waste of time.

LETTING GO OF THE LITTLE THINGS

Nothing will sap your strength more than dwelling on things that don't matter. Worrying about a friend who doesn't reply to a text message, or the driver who cuts you up on your way to work, is a waste of valuable time, energy and brainpower. Obsessing over trivial things won't accomplish anything other than making you tired and irritable. Save your energy for accomplishing what matters – whether that is being there for a family member, running a successful business or collecting money for a charitable cause. It will take conscious effort and practice, but you can train yourself to let go of the little things and focus your energy on what you can control. Don't let negative energy weigh you down and prevent you from reaching your full potential.

CREATIVE SOLUTIONS

If your path is blocked, create an alternative route. Creativity is your ultimate weapon. For example, if you want to meditate but 'don't have time', practise mindfulness in the shower each morning. If you want to learn French but can't afford tuition, listen to an audio language lesson when you exercise. If you want to start saving but 'can't afford it', start putting £5 aside every month. Whenever you hit an obstacle, find a creative way to climb over it or go around it. Never let it stop you.

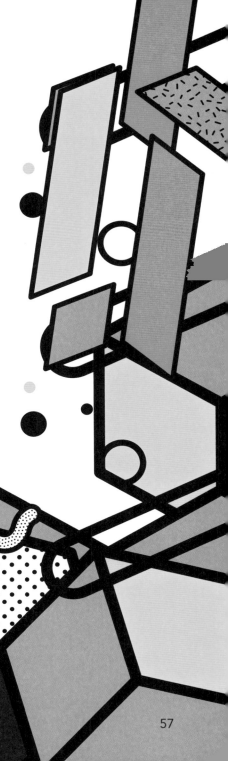

YOU ARE NOT YOUR THOUGHTS

I HAVE NEVER HAD TO FACE ANYTHING THAT COULD OVERWHELM THE NATIVE OPTIMISM AND STUBBORN PERSEVERANCE I WAS BLESSED WITH.

Sonia Sotomayor

FOCUS ON YOUR PROGRESS, NOT YOUR GOALS

By fixating on goals, you only see the gap between where you currently are and where you would like to be. Instead, focus on the progress you are making. Training for a marathon? See how much quicker you were than last week! Writing a book? That's two chapters completed today! When you are not concentrating on the disparity between targets and reality, you can really celebrate all your small victories – and your final goals will take care of themselves.

RETHINK STRESS

Begin to see stress as a professional athlete views their workout – as an opportunity to grow stronger. Stress builds character – it tests your resolve and problem-solving abilities. Look at it as a workout for your mind. Or turn it into a game and challenge yourself: how calmly can you steer through life, despite the bumps in the road? Viewing stress in a more positive light can help you embrace life's challenges and obstacles.

ACCENTUATE THE POSITIVES

Just because you believe something, doesn't make it true. Many beliefs that we have held for years – often since childhood – sabotage our resilience. Start challenging the beliefs that are holding you back. Psychologists recommend judging your beliefs on four criteria. Firstly, look at the evidence. Does it support or negate your belief? If you begin to question your worth, focus on the evidence that disputes this. Secondly, consider the alternatives. Rather than latching on to the bleakest explanation for a bad event, find a more positive explanation. Thirdly, what are the implications? When faced with a setback, try not to draw negative conclusions. And finally, think about usefulness. Question the utility of your beliefs – even the most negative situations can have hidden gifts in the end. So, whenever you recognise beliefs that are holding you back, try replacing them with new, more empowering ones.

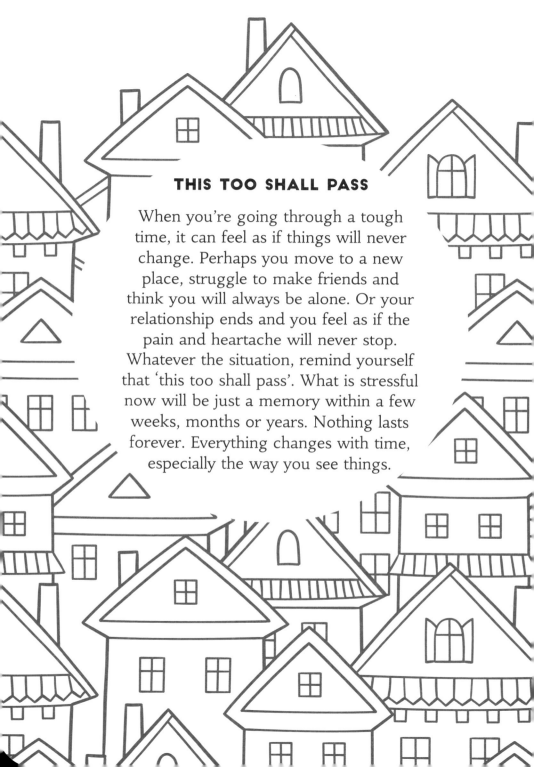

THIS TOO SHALL PASS

When you're going through a tough time, it can feel as if things will never change. Perhaps you move to a new place, struggle to make friends and think you will always be alone. Or your relationship ends and you feel as if the pain and heartache will never stop. Whatever the situation, remind yourself that 'this too shall pass'. What is stressful now will be just a memory within a few weeks, months or years. Nothing lasts forever. Everything changes with time, especially the way you see things.

CULTIVATE COMPASSION

When faced with a setback, it's all too easy to be hard on ourselves – but that won't help one bit. If you have a cigarette after quitting, or fail to stick to a new study regime, beating yourself up is likely to start a downward spiral that can be hard to escape from. Instead, practise self-compassion. Remind yourself that you actually made an effort. Treat yourself with kindness, climb back in the saddle and keep going.

Success is not final, failure is not fatal:

it is the

courage
to
continue

that counts.

Winston Churchill

CHANGE YOUR THOUGHTS AND YOU CHANGE YOUR WORLD.

Norman Vincent Peale

PRACTISE BEING STRAIGHTFORWARD AND ASSERTIVE

Agreeing to unreasonable or unrealistic demands only sets you up for failure and increases your stress levels. Don't be afraid of saying no – be assertive and make your voice heard.

You are a song
– make sure you're heard

TAKE PRIDE IN
YOUR ACHIEVEMENTS

Give yourself credit where it
is due – stop to tell yourself 'well
done' if you've completed a task you've
been avoiding, or you've successfully
navigated a tough week at work. Treat
yourself to something sweet or your
favourite dinner, a homemade spa
night in your bathroom or watching
your favourite film – any activity
that feels like a reward
for your efforts.

FORTITUDE IS THE GUARD AND SUPPORT OF THE OTHER VIRTUES.

John Locke

DON'T ASSUME THE WORST

If your mind is racing and you are consumed with worry, are you scaring yourself with 'what ifs'? Imagined scenarios may seem incredibly real but they are a figment of our imagination. A large proportion of the things we imagine never actually happen. Let's say you take your dog to the vet because he has stopped

eating, and you spend the day before the appointment worrying that the vet will discover a terrible disease. In reality, the vet finds a splinter in the dog's gum and removes it, solving the problem. Yet you spent the previous day gripped with anxiety. Worrying serves no purpose other than making you feel anxious.

Show the world what you're made of. You're tougher than you think.

Live today,

for tomorrow it will all be history.

Proverb

RESILIENCE IS ORDINARY

Millions of people across the world display resilience every day. It is not exclusive to the powerful, the high-flying or the rich. Resilience is achievable and can be used by anyone, even in the smallest of ways.

Life happens.
Let it be.

STOP WITH THE WHAT-IFS

When things go wrong it can be easy to let your thoughts run wild. Constantly imagining the very worst possible scenario or outcome is something psychologists call 'catastrophising'. For example, let's say you miss a deadline at work. This sets off a chain reaction of negative thinking in which you see yourself being fired, not being able to get another job, unable to provide for yourself and your family and maybe even losing your home. As soon as you realise you are overreacting like this, take a step back from your thoughts. Challenge how logical they are. It might help to put your thoughts on to paper. Does missing one deadline on one occasion really mean you will be instantly fired and never able to find another job? Or is the reality that you have performed well in the past and are well respected at work, meaning your manager is more likely to offer you some training or feedback than anything as harsh as even a disciplinary? Stopping yourself from catastrophising takes a lot of conscious effort, but if you continually challenge your irrational thoughts, you will feel less demoralised and will be motivated to take action to make things better.

You are the hero of your story

CONNECT WITH PEOPLE

Maintaining good relationships
with family, friends and colleagues
is essential. A strong support
network can help you bounce
back from setbacks, provide a
friendly ear and share in your
goals and successes. Your
support network is the solid
ground from which you can
propel yourself upwards.

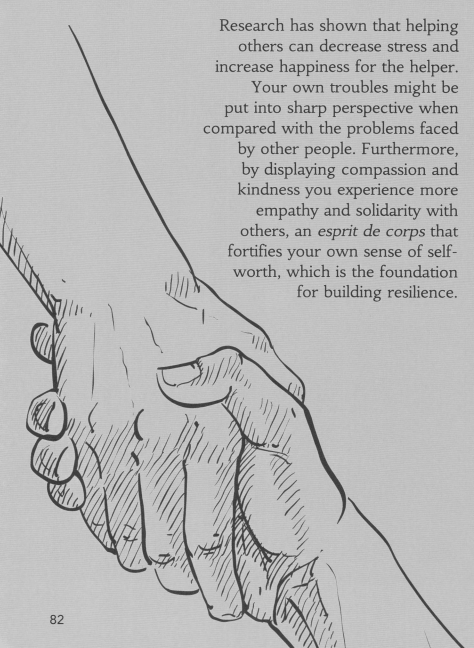

HELP OTHERS

Research has shown that helping others can decrease stress and increase happiness for the helper. Your own troubles might be put into sharp perspective when compared with the problems faced by other people. Furthermore, by displaying compassion and kindness you experience more empathy and solidarity with others, an *esprit de corps* that fortifies your own sense of self-worth, which is the foundation for building resilience.

Together we are stronger

MiLk

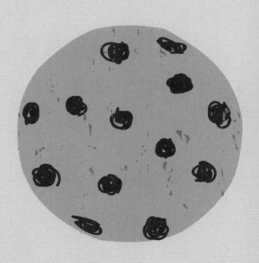

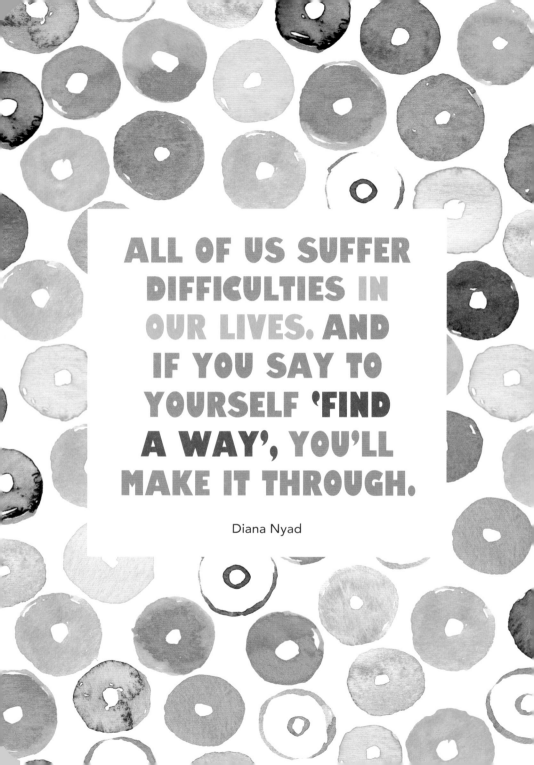

ALL OF US SUFFER DIFFICULTIES IN OUR LIVES. AND IF YOU SAY TO YOURSELF 'FIND A WAY', YOU'LL MAKE IT THROUGH.

Diana Nyad

LESSONS IN FAILURE

No one is immune to failure. We all experience disappointments, frustrations and bruised egos from time to time. However, resilient people don't let failure stop them. They use the lessons hidden within these difficult moments to help them overcome their next challenge. If you've made a mistake or something's gone disastrously wrong, take a little bit of time to reflect. Ask yourself some constructive questions. What did I do right? What could I have done better? What's the lesson here? Entrepreneurs, scientists, inventors and leaders all know there can be no success without failure. Most people experience catastrophes in some form or other, including financial problems, breakdowns and relationships ending. Successful souls manage to pick themselves up and persevere, armed with greater knowledge and wisdom.

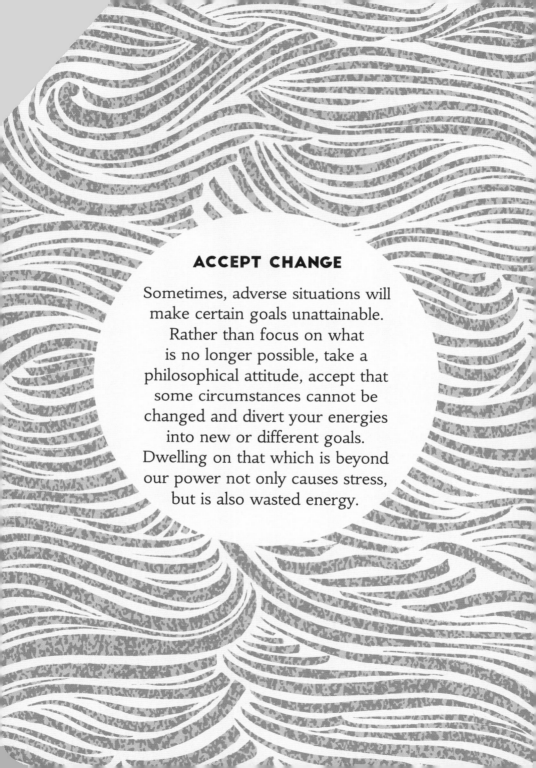

ACCEPT CHANGE

Sometimes, adverse situations will make certain goals unattainable. Rather than focus on what is no longer possible, take a philosophical attitude, accept that some circumstances cannot be changed and divert your energies into new or different goals. Dwelling on that which is beyond our power not only causes stress, but is also wasted energy.

Welcome

today's

challenges

Every change brings

opportunity

WAYS TO BRING RESILIENCE INTO YOUR LIFE

MAKE every MINUTE COUNT

PRACTISE GRATITUDE

Taking time to acknowledge what
is good in your life can make all the
difference when adversity strikes. Studies
show that gratitude lifts our spirits
and floods our body with feel-good
hormones. How you practise gratitude
is up to you. You could end each day by
reflecting on all the things that went well,
or you could look for things that make
you smile as you go about your day

(such as an unexpected hug or bumping
into an old friend). Some people find
it useful to have a dedicated gratitude
journal in which they write down
three things they are grateful for every
morning or evening. By training your
mind to notice what's right in life
rather than what's wrong, you'll have
more emotional strength reserves
to tap into to help you bounce back
from the stresses and strains of life.

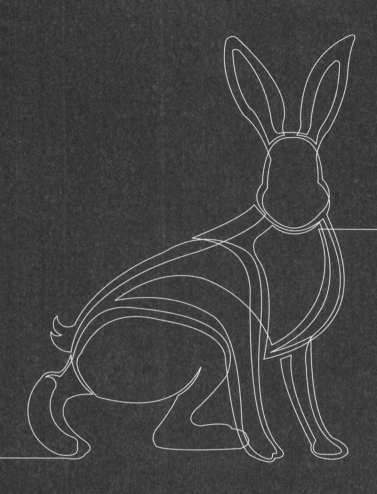

PUT YOUR EAR DOWN
CLOSE TO YOUR SOUL
AND LISTEN HARD.

Anne Sexton

EXTRAORDINARY LIVES

The bigger your dreams and goals, the more likely it is that you will face hurdles along the way. When this happens, will you give up or persevere? A simple way to strengthen your inner resolve is to read about other people who have overcome great odds. From famous figures such as Winston Churchill and Rosa Parks to lesser-known heroes throughout the arts and sciences, seek out true-life stories of courage and resilience and draw strength from their examples.

CHANGE YOUR ABC

Many of us believe that negative events cause us to behave in a certain way, but research reveals that our reactions are based on our individual thoughts about adversity. This explains why people respond differently to the same stressful situation. A person might experience adversity (A) in the form of their partner leaving them. They might then have the belief (B) that they are worthless. As a consequence (C), they would sink into despair and find it hard to summon the motivation to go out and meet new people. But another person in the same situation might recognise that their relationship hadn't been working for quite some time and feel they are now free to meet someone who is right for them. They might feel sad about the relationship ending, but they would be optimistic about their future and might decide to join some local clubs to widen their social circle. Reflecting carefully on the ABCs in your life will help you overcome difficulties rather than letting them overwhelm you.

DIFFICULTIES ARE THINGS THAT SHOW A PERSON WHAT THEY ARE.

Epictetus

LISTEN TO YOUR INNER VOICE

AFFIRM YOUR STRENGTH

As the saying goes, 'What you think is what you become.' A powerful way to boost your confidence and fortitude is to repeat affirmations of strength to yourself. Experiment with different statements until you find one that resonates with you. For example, 'I am strong, whole and complete,' or, 'I can face any challenge.' Repeat your affirmation quietly or silently to yourself at intervals throughout the day and whenever you face a setback or difficulty.

WHATEVER WORKS FOR YOU

Everyone is on their own path when developing resilience. If you find one strategy works better than another, then use it! We are all different and what is useful for one person may not be of much help to another. Don't be afraid to experiment with different techniques or to admit when something isn't working for you.

BE PART OF SOMETHING BIGGER

Spiritual beliefs can be a source of great strength in life. Whether you are religious or not, strengthening your connection to something bigger – such as a god, nature or the universe – can both comfort and inspire you during dark times. Make time for contemplative practices such as prayer, meditation or spending time in nature. Studies show that people who are spiritual tend to be more emotionally resilient.

HELP SOMEONE ELSE

Volunteering can be a great way to distance yourself from your troubles. It will shift your focus from yourself to others and can help you put things into perspective. You could volunteer regularly at a food bank, or simply look for opportunities to help a neighbour, friend or colleague. Studies show that volunteering reduces depression, increases happiness and self-esteem, and boosts our sense of being in control of our lives.

LET IT OUT

Honour your feelings and recognise that difficult
emotions such as anger, depression and loneliness
are a natural part of the human experience. Let
your emotions out by having a good cry if you
need to. Crying can help you to regain your
emotional balance as it releases toxins that have
built up in the body due to stress. You should find
that you feel calmer and less anxious afterwards.

Another good way to express your feelings is through a creative outlet such as painting, blogging or playing a musical instrument. Creative activities can reduce stress and help you to process your experiences and feelings. The options for self-expression are endless. Whether you write poems, take photographs or draw sketches, creative pursuits offer you the space to deal with a range of emotions in a healthy and constructive way. Find something that gives you release.

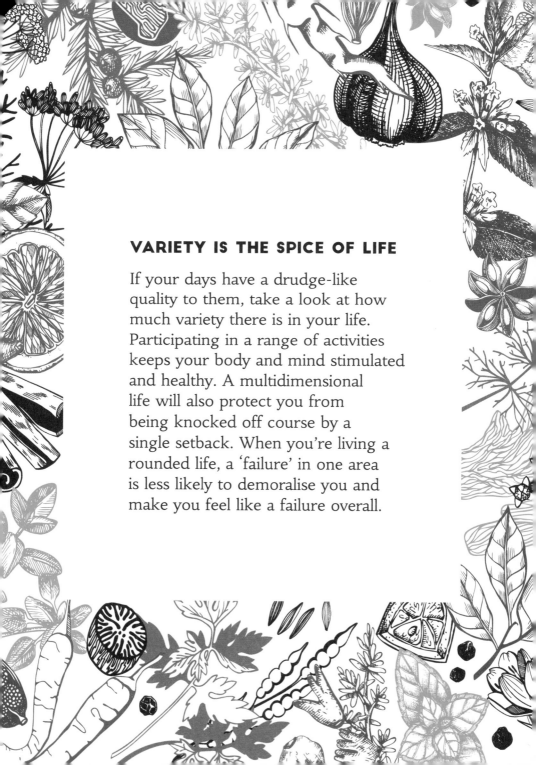

VARIETY IS THE SPICE OF LIFE

If your days have a drudge-like quality to them, take a look at how much variety there is in your life. Participating in a range of activities keeps your body and mind stimulated and healthy. A multidimensional life will also protect you from being knocked off course by a single setback. When you're living a rounded life, a 'failure' in one area is less likely to demoralise you and make you feel like a failure overall.

TRANSFORM PAIN INTO POWER

The first step to becoming resilient is realising that any pain or adversity that you face can be converted into the fuel that propels you forward. Rather than allowing negative experiences to bury you, use them to climb upwards. Adversity is something to aim at and to smash through on the way to achieving your goals.

WORDS OF INSPIRATION

Sometimes a comforting or positive word is all we need to motivate us to keep going. Consider keeping a book of inspirational quotes on your bedside table or in your bag, so you can dip into it on a regular basis. You could also write out your favourite uplifting quotes and put them in your wallet or on a bathroom mirror where you can see them every day.

OPEN
CURTAINS
A NEW
DAY

THE
AND LET
BEGIN!

LOOK AT THE BIGGER PICTURE

When you're going through a rough patch, try going outside at night and gazing up in awe at the stars. Reflect on the fact that you are a tiny speck on a beautiful planet in a universe of a hundred thousand million stars (that's '1' with 29 zeros after it!). Viewing your life as part of a bigger picture can put your problems into perspective and help you face challenges with renewed strength.

Seeing the bigger picture opens your eyes to what is the truth.

Wadada Leo Smith

BABY STEPS

When faced with challenges in life, we can become paralysed with fear. Whether it's a big challenge, such as starting a new business, or a smaller challenge, such as starting a fitness regime, the key to success is to face fear and take action. The easiest way to do this is to take baby steps. Pick one thing you're currently procrastinating about and think of at least five ways to take a step in the right direction.

For example, if your goal is to get fit, you could begin with the baby step of doing five push-ups or squats a day, or going for a 10-minute walk on your lunch break. Don't be put off by the size of the step. Small steps lead to big results over time. With each new step, your confidence and enthusiasm will grow. Keep moving towards your goal. Resilient people take action.

The purpose of life is to enjoy it

THINK POSITIVE

Positive thinking can aid in stress management and even improve your general health and well-being. You don't have to ignore the bad things or bury your head in the sand; instead it involves making the best of bad situations, seeing what positives can be drawn from difficult events and putting faith in your ability to overcome them.

ASK YOURSELF 'WHY'?

One of the key ways to challenge negative thoughts that drain your confidence is to ask 'why'? For example, the commonly held negative thought that 'I'm not good enough' can make you worried about many aspects of your life. Perhaps you feel you are not good enough at your job, not good enough in your studies, not a good enough friend, not a good enough partner. Now is the time to ask yourself why that is: can you find five actual reasons why you are not good enough? It is unlikely you can. Let logic prevail – if the only way you can answer this simple question is with 'because I know it's true' or with minor incidents from the past, you can begin to change your self-perception.

We don't even know
how strong we are
until we are forced
to bring that hidden
strength forward.

Isabel Allende

Look at life from unexpected angles today

USE MANTRAS

A mantra is a positive phrase that you repeat to yourself, confirming your positive thoughts and affirmations, such as 'I am' or 'I will' instead of 'I can't'. Mantras can be thought or said out loud. Many people believe that actually saying your mantra out loud

makes it more effective,
as vocalising something
gives it more substance.
You can also write down
your chosen mantra
and put it somewhere
you are likely to see it,
such as the kitchen wall
or bathroom mirror.
Regularly repeating your
chosen mantra will help
you reaffirm your faith in
yourself and your abilities.

MAKE A HAPPY LIST

In order to focus on the positive, try making a list of all the good things in your life. This might seem difficult at first, but you can always ask friends and family for help. The list could be made up of personal or general points, for example 'I am healthy', or, 'My family is supportive'. This is something you can pin in a prominent place to remind you of the good around you when negativity seems to be creeping in.

ACT AS IF YOU HAVE AMPLE CONFIDENCE

Vividly imagine how your life would be if you were naturally confident right now. How would your posture be? How would you move? How would your voice sound? What would you say to yourself? What would you picture in your mind? Once you have a clear image, imagine you are this person. Step into their shoes, see the world through their eyes and feel what they feel. If you do this often, you'll forget that you're acting and confidence will become a habit.

Grab a double helping of *life,* with a side-order of *adventure.*

A GOOD HALF

OF THE ART OF LIVING IS

RESILIENCE.

Alain de Botton

THE MAGIC OF SOLITUDE

There is so much pressure to be active and busy that it can be hard to justify spending time alone 'doing nothing'. However, periods of solitude can play a crucial part in building your emotional resilience. Time alone gives you a chance to stop and reflect. It allows you to tune in to who you are and what matters most to you. It encourages self-reliance and a feeling of being in the driving seat, rather than your life being controlled by external demands. Try taking regular time out for solitude, even if it's only five minutes a day to begin with. Meditate for a few minutes in the morning, eat your lunch in the park, listen to soothing music, or sit by a fire and gaze into the flames. Make a point of setting aside time for rest and reflection and see how much better you feel.

When
life
throws
tomatoes
at you,
make a
Bloody
Mary!

WHY NOT live

A LIFE?

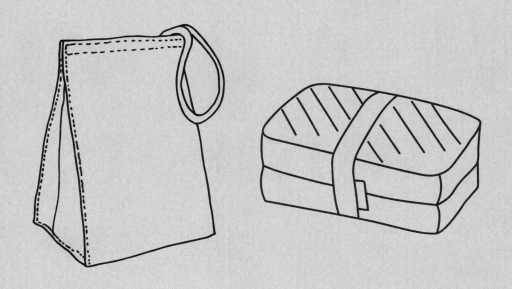

BE PREPARED FOR THE DAY AHEAD

The pressure of deadlines, meetings, phone calls and long working hours can all build up and cause us to doubt our ability to handle things, which can upset confidence levels. This is likely to not only get in the way of an enjoyable, effective working life, but can also have a negative impact on the rest of your life. A simple way to reduce this feeling of pressure is to plan

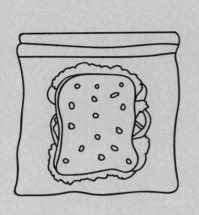

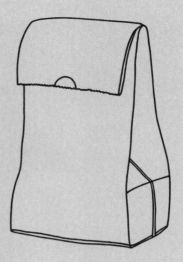

and prepare for your working day. Pack your lunch the night before so that you are not rushing to put it together in the morning. Look up bus or train times in advance to ensure you know about any delays, and make a list of the tasks you wish to complete, so when you get to your place of work your day is already planned out. Taking these steps can give you more confidence in your workload management.

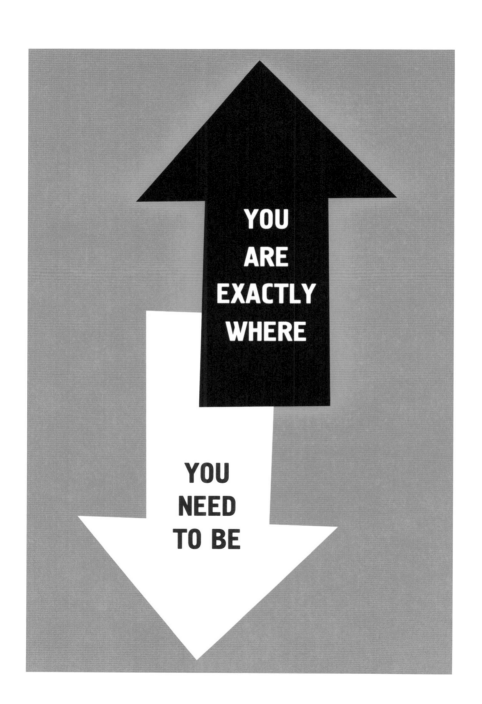

A RESILIENT BODY

POWER POSE

Two minutes standing in 'power pose' can dramatically alter your brain chemistry. Try adopting a wide stance with your hands up in the air, as if you've just won the lottery or your football team has scored a goal. Alternatively, try the 'Wonder Woman' pose, with

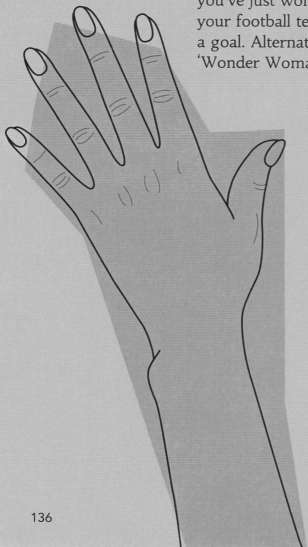

your feet hip-distance apart and your hands on your hips. While you might not want to do this in the middle of the office or at college, you can quickly do this in the toilets or when no one's about whenever you need an instant confidence boost.

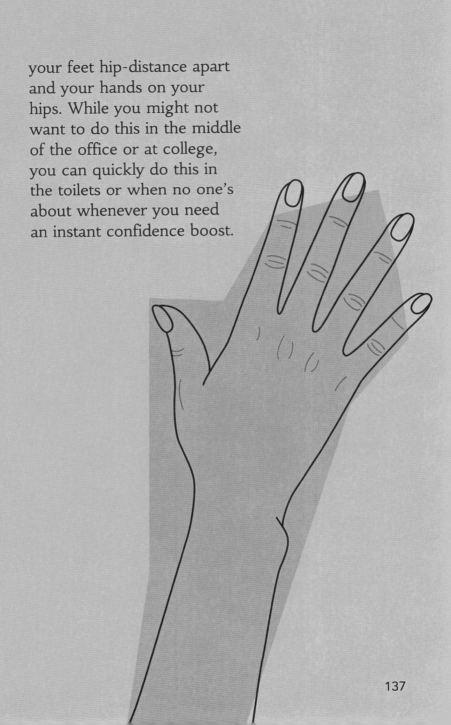

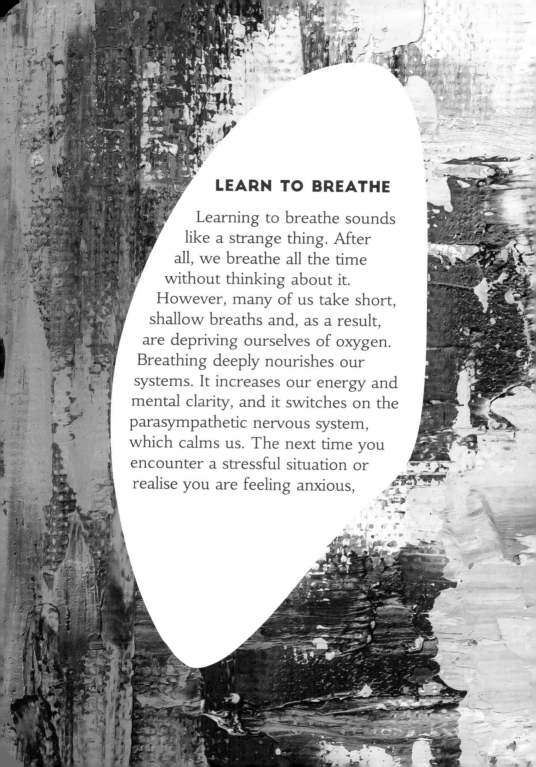

LEARN TO BREATHE

Learning to breathe sounds like a strange thing. After all, we breathe all the time without thinking about it. However, many of us take short, shallow breaths and, as a result, are depriving ourselves of oxygen. Breathing deeply nourishes our systems. It increases our energy and mental clarity, and it switches on the parasympathetic nervous system, which calms us. The next time you encounter a stressful situation or realise you are feeling anxious,

place your hand on your
stomach and take a deep
breath into your navel, letting
your body relax and fill with air.
Then exhale s-l-o-w-l-y. Repeat
five times or until you feel calm.
Several times throughout the day,
tune in to your breathing. Is your
stomach clenched? Are you taking
shallow breaths from your chest?
Are you holding your breath? If
so, practise a few rounds of deep
breathing. If done regularly, this
will gently retrain your body to
breathe correctly.

One way to break up any kind of tension is

good, deep breathing.

Byron Nelson

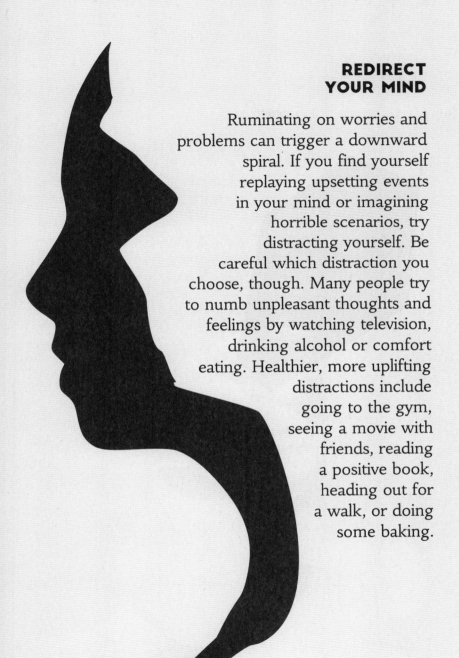

REDIRECT YOUR MIND

Ruminating on worries and problems can trigger a downward spiral. If you find yourself replaying upsetting events in your mind or imagining horrible scenarios, try distracting yourself. Be careful which distraction you choose, though. Many people try to numb unpleasant thoughts and feelings by watching television, drinking alcohol or comfort eating. Healthier, more uplifting distractions include going to the gym, seeing a movie with friends, reading a positive book, heading out for a walk, or doing some baking.

LOOK AFTER YOURSELF

Work, family, friends – you probably find you expend a lot of energy on these groups of people. Don't forget to take care of yourself. There's no reason to feel guilty about turning down overtime at work, or missing a social event, if it allows you to recharge your batteries or catch up on some well-deserved relaxation time. Stretching yourself too thin can be exhausting, and resilient people know that by taking some time out you can come at life feeling refreshed and positive.

GIVE YOUR BODY THE BEST CHANCE TO BE RESILIENT

It's no secret that a healthy body leads to a healthy mind so help build your resilience through eating healthily. Don't get bogged down with dieting, instead aim to stabilise your blood-sugar levels as this will help you to produce the feel-good hormone serotonin. Eat regularly, starting the day with a good low-GI (Glycemic Index) breakfast with slow-release energy – such as porridge or muesli – to maintain your energy levels and top up with healthy snacks such as fruit and nuts. Aim for a balanced diet with a good mix of fruit, vegetables and protein, and go easy on the carbs. Don't eat too late into the evening and aim for lower fat, magnesium-rich foods such as fish and leafy green vegetables as these will help with getting a good night's rest too.

TIME FOR BED

Sleep keeps us both mentally and physically strong. Just one night of bad sleep can cause us to feel negative, irritable and more easily overwhelmed the next day. Most adults need at least 7–8 hours' sleep a night but everyone is different. If you wake up feeling refreshed, you're probably getting enough sleep. If you're not getting enough sleep, the following tips will help:

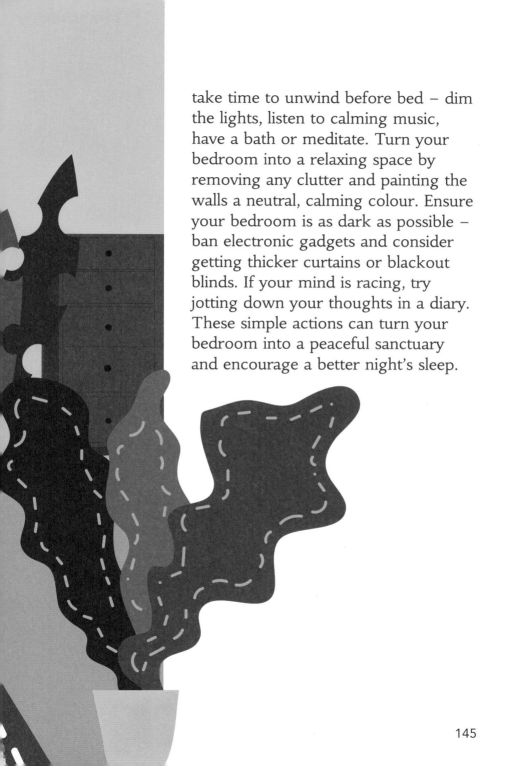

take time to unwind before bed – dim the lights, listen to calming music, have a bath or meditate. Turn your bedroom into a relaxing space by removing any clutter and painting the walls a neutral, calming colour. Ensure your bedroom is as dark as possible – ban electronic gadgets and consider getting thicker curtains or blackout blinds. If your mind is racing, try jotting down your thoughts in a diary. These simple actions can turn your bedroom into a peaceful sanctuary and encourage a better night's sleep.

EXERCISING YOUR WAY TO RESILIENCE

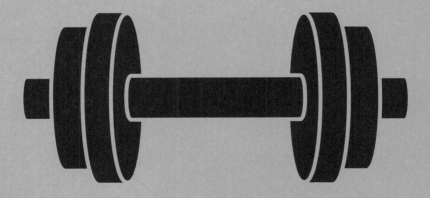

You're only one workout away from a good mood

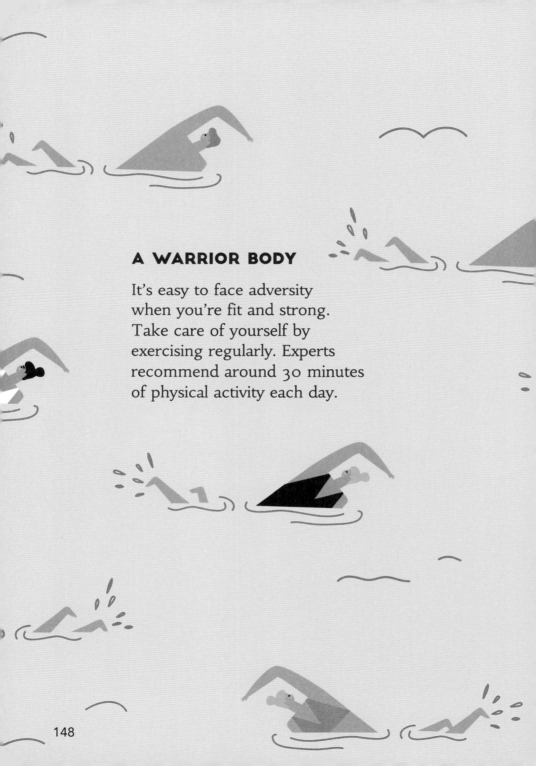

A WARRIOR BODY

It's easy to face adversity
when you're fit and strong.
Take care of yourself by
exercising regularly. Experts
recommend around 30 minutes
of physical activity each day.

Exercise helps build resilience in several ways: it produces endorphins and serotonin which lift your spirits, and it changes the way your brain responds to stress, making it more resistant to anxiety. It can also increase your energy, boost your confidence and promote better sleep, all of which will help you bounce back from stressful situations. The best way to start a fitness regime is to experiment with different exercises and activities until you find something you really enjoy. Any activity counts if it raises your heart rate and makes you breathe faster and feel warmer, whether it's brisk walking, dancing, rollerblading or swimming. Signing up for a team sport or exercise class, or exercising with a friend, can motivate you to stick with it and work harder. It also makes getting fit more fun!

NATURE'S MEDICINE

Make walking and being outside in nature a regular part of your routine. The fresh air, exercise and contact with nature are guaranteed to raise your spirits. Studies show just five minutes in a green space can reduce blood pressure and a 20- to 30-minute walk can have the same calming effect as a mild tranquiliser. Besides walking, there are lots of other ways to connect with nature. If you have a garden, get outside and do some simple weeding. If you don't have a garden, why not try volunteering with a local conservation group?

YOGIC LIFE

The benefits of yoga go
far beyond improving
physical flexibility.
Yoga can help you
sleep better. It
can stabilise
your mood and
reduce stress
and anxiety.
Challenging poses
in particular can help you build confidence and
inner strength, which can positively affect the rest
of your life. There are lots of different styles
of yoga, which means there's a class
to suit everybody.

BUILD YOUR COPING RESOURCES

Mentally strong people recognise they won't be able to combat stress if they're worn out and running on empty. They take regular time out to relax and recharge their batteries. Consider taking up meditation, yoga, t'ai chi or some other relaxation technique. These activities will help you unwind after a stressful day and remain calm during times of stress in the future. Taking time out isn't self-indulgent – it's an essential strategy for coping with the ups and downs of life. Problems are easier to overcome from a state of relaxation.

All great
achievements
require time.

Maya Angelou

SWIM TOWARDS A MORE RESILIENT YOU

Swimming is one of the most effective forms of exercise, both in terms of giving you a full body workout and in allowing you to relax and unwind. The rhythmic lap of the water with each stroke, and the focus on your technique and breathing, really make this a great way to move your mind away from your worries, allowing some quality time to yourself. This alone time can give you a chance to reflect on the positive changes you are making. Add to that the fact that floating in water is a wonderfully soothing experience and you've got a perfect recipe for resilience-boosting relaxation.

SHAKE IT OFF

Dancing is, for many people, one of the most fun ways to get fit and – alongside releasing the mood-boosting endorphins exercise provides – it's a great positivity cocktail. It can be as simple as putting on your favourite music at home and dancing around your living room or bedroom, or you could try a class. Jive, jazz, ballroom and Latin dance classes are all great ways to get fit and meet new people, and fitness fusion classes such as Zumba are becoming ever-more popular. Choose a style that suits you and, above all, enjoy it.

MAN NEVER MADE ANY MATERIAL AS RESILIENT

AS THE HUMAN SPIRIT.

Bernard Williams

If you're interested in finding out more about our books,
find us on Facebook at Summersdale Publishers
and follow us on Twitter at @Summersdale.

WWW.SUMMERSDALE.COM

IMAGE CREDITS

p.5 © Alexander_P/Shutterstock.com; p.7 © Sudowoodo/Shutterstock.com; pp.8–9, pp.138–139 (background) © Sweet Art/Shutterstock.com; pp.10–11 © Elina Li/Shutterstock.com; p.12 © dobrodzei/Shutterstock.com; p.13 © Aleks Melnik/Shutterstock.com; p.14 © Ivengo/Shutterstock.com; pp.16–17 © 7 pips/Shutterstock.com; p.19 © SAHAS2015/Shutterstock.com; p.20 © Lucy Ya/Shutterstock.com; p.22 © RFV/Shutterstock.com; p.24 © Zubdash/Shutterstock.com; p.25 © Svetlana Drujinina/Shutterstock.com; p.26 © Grinbox/Shutterstock.com; pp.28–29 © grop/Shutterstock.com; p.30 © HappyAprilBoy/Shutterstock.com; p.34 © koyash07/Shutterstock.com; p.36 © Petrovic Igor/Shutterstock.com; p.37 © tinkivinki/Shutterstock.com; p.38 © solmariart/Shutterstock.com; pp.39, 61 © Dmitry Guzhanin/Shutterstock.com; p.42 © Shutterclub/Shutterstock.com; p.43 (groceries) © Franzi/Shutterstock.com, (bag) © nikiteev_konstantin/Shutterstock.com; pp.44–45 © Kapitosh/Shutterstock.com; p.46 (background) © PASAKORN RANGSIYANONT/Shutterstock.com, (text) © Tortuga/Shutterstock.com; p.47 © RYGER/Shutterstock.com; pp.48–49 © Artlusy/Shutterstock.com; p.50 © silm/Shutterstock.com; p.51 © lisima/Shutterstock.com; pp.52–53 © kotyplastic/Shutterstock.com; pp.54, 55, 58, 74, 123 © Yurta/Shutterstock.com; p.60 © Franzi/Shutterstock.com; p.63 © Drawlab19/Shutterstock.com; p.64 © likemuzzy/Shutterstock.com; p.65 © zorina_larisa/Shutterstock.com; p.66 © Little Princess/Shutterstock.com; p.67 © milsamil/Shutterstock.com; p.68 © Helga Khorimarko/Shutterstock.com; p.69 © Giraffarte/Shutterstock.com; p.70 (background) © Magenta10/Shutterstock.com, (illustration) © Olly Molly/Shutterstock.com; p.71 © Login/Shutterstock.com; pp.72–73, 75, 76, 77, 84, 87, 100, 101, 102–103, 108–109, 112–113 (background), 114, 119, 148–149, 150, 156, 158–159 © Tasiania/Shutterstock.com; pp.78–79 © KA-KA/Shutterstock.com; p.80 © ankudi/Shutterstock.com; p.81 © igor kisselev/Shutterstock.com; p.82 © first vector trend/Shutterstock.com; p.83 © S-Victoria/Shutterstock.com; p.85 © Jemastock/Shutterstock.com; p.86 © CPD-Lab/Shutterstock.com; pp.88, 93, 118 © Oleksandr Shatokhin/Shutterstock.com; p.89 © EgudinKa/Shutterstock.com; p.90 © Tiwat K/Shutterstock.com; p.91 © nuvrenia/Shutterstock.com; p.92 © Spring Bine/Shutterstock.com; p.95 © Cristian Amoretti/Shutterstock.com; p.96 © INAMEL/Shutterstock.com; pp.97, 98, 99, 155 © lineartestpilot/Shutterstock.com; p.104 © geraria/Shutterstock.com; p.105 © andrewvect/Shutterstock.com; pp.106–107 © Pylypchuk/Shutterstock.com; p.110 © Anna Kutukova/Shutterstock.com; p.111 © Natalia Mikhaleva/Shutterstock.com; p.112 (footprints) © NeMaria/Shutterstock.com; p.113 (birds) © Ihnatovich Maryia/Shutterstock.com; pp.116–117 © NomadSoul/Shutterstock.com; pp.120–121 © Marina Demidova/Shutterstock.com; p.122 © AllNikArt/Shutterstock.com; pp.124–125 © Bluehousestudio/Shutterstock.com; p.126 © lecosta/Shutterstock.com; pp.128–129 © flowerstock/Shutterstock.com; p.130 © katyalitvin/Shutterstock.com; p.131 © Lera Efremova/Shutterstock.com; pp.132–133 © Koto Moto/Shutterstock.com; p.134 © Tanor/Shutterstock.com; p.135 © MarijaPiliponyte/Shutterstock.com; pp.136–137 © Val_Iva/Shutterstock.com; pp.138–139 (lungs) © Julia Lipatova/Shutterstock.com; p.140 © MIKHAIL GRACHIKOV/Shutterstock.com; p.141 © GrAl/Shutterstock.com; p.142 © GoodStudio/Shutterstock.com; p.143 © Kudryashka/Shutterstock.com; pp.144–145 © gigirosado/Shutterstock.com; p.146 © M-vector/Shutterstock.com; p.147 © aquamarine painter/Shutterstock.com; p.151 © Oleh Markov/Shutterstock.com; pp.152–153 © Chief Crow Daria/Shutterstock.com; p.154 © Isaeva Anna/Shutterstock.com; p.157 © RetroClipArt/Shutterstock.com

Every reasonable effort has been made by the publisher to trace and acknowledge the copyright holders of material used in this book. If any errors or omissions are brought to light, the publisher will endeavour to rectify them in any reprints or future editions.